Finger Puppets, Fing

Contents

Snail Walk

One snail,
two snails
had a little talk.
Three snails,
four snails
took a little walk.
Five snails,
six snails
climbed a pile of bricks.
Then a big, black bird
flew down
and gobbled up all six.

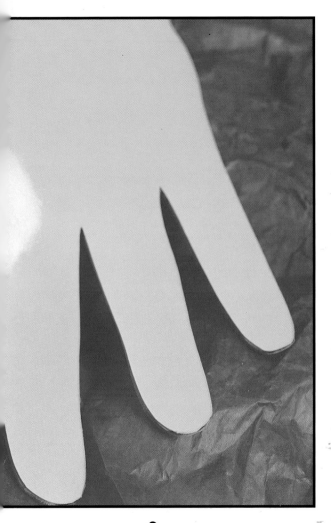

3

For a snail, you will need:

1. Paint the body brown.

2. Glue on the "shell" and eyes.

For a bird, you will need:

1. Paint the body black.

2. Glue on feathers,
   face, and eyes.

Five Little Mice

Five little mice
sat down to spin.
Cat went by,
and he looked in.

"What are you doing,
my five little men?"

"We're making coats
for gentlemen."

"Shall I come in and
bite off your threads?"

"Oh no, Cat, you'll bite
off our heads."

6

For a mouse, you will need:

1. Paint the body grey.

2. Glue on the face, eyes, and tail.

For a cat, you will need:

1. Paint stripes on body.

2. Glue on the face.

Buzzing Bees

Here is the beehive.
Where are the bees?
Hiding away
where nobody sees?
Look!
Now they're coming
out of the hive.
One, two,
three, four, five.
Buzz! Buzz! Buzz!
Back to the hive!

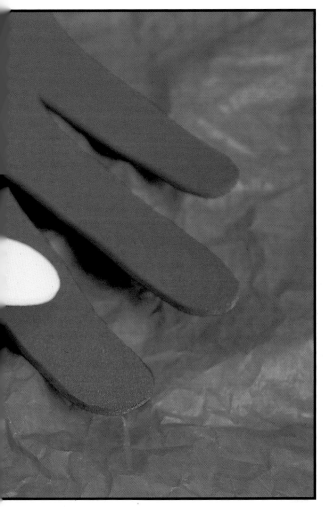

For a bee, you will need:

1. Paint the body yellow.

2. Draw stripes and glue wings on the body.

3. Glue on eyes and
antennae.

For a beehive, you will
need paint and cardboard.

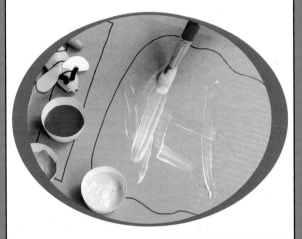

13

Five Little Rabbits

This little rabbit likes cabbage.

This little rabbit likes clover.

This little rabbit likes carrots.

This little rabbit rolls over.

And this little rabbit goes

lippety-loppety

all the way home to mother.

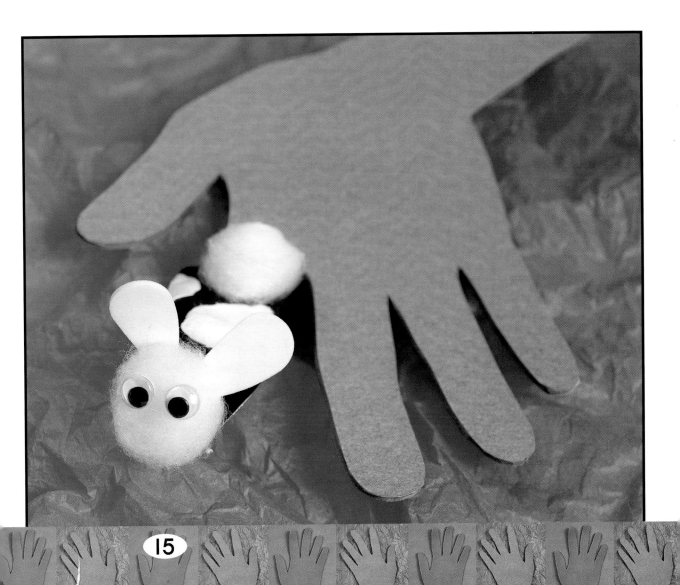

For a rabbit, you will need:

2. Glue on cotton balls.

1. Paint the body.

3. Glue on eyes and ears.